The Prayer of the Hypocrite

The Prayer of the Hypocrite

NATASHA RAY JAMES I

Welcome to the depths of my mind's abyss

Table of Contents

The Prayer of the Hypocrite

Acceptance

No one knew the Czar would fall like this
disgraceful

For many years, the Czar played with his mustache
dangling his fingers inside his beard
and for many years, his people tried to do the same
yet, they had no mustache
they had no beard

The Czar did not cry on the day of his ousting
instead, he shaved himself bare
commensurate with his people
and servants

The Czar drank his vodka
staring into the mirror

His reflection told no lies
confronting his own self
without the mustache
without the beard

There he sat
once the Czar
he was

drinking vodka
with the company of his bare reflection

The Wait Was Over

And the angels came no sooner
and left no later than they had to
see,
they were the punctual type
see,
because God asked them to be
Now,
the angels were dressed in white
of course
That is the way angels should be dressed
according to her
They waved their wings around
and a golden glow framed their halos
as expected
That is the way angels should be floating
according to her
Not once did she say a word to the angels
see,
this would be unmannered
Maybe even unholy
The angels talked about this
and of that
and, indeed, they began to bore her
but she kept quiet
see,
Because these were angels after all

Dr. Kevorkian

It took but no time at all
to understand that my death was nearing
and the glee
and the impatience
to greet my demise
became oh so overwhelming
the clock ticked slower
as if to jest
and with each stroke of the hand
my mind succumbed to the delirium further
and with each stroke of the hand
darkness enveloped my vision
the ticking continued
till

Becoming

It wasn't so long ago
when a thought became a seed

And so laid the seed within the dirt
provoking tempting fantasies for the earth's worms

Came rain on a late winter day
when the air proved warm
and the seed took notice

Beginning to sprout, the worms slithered toward it
but had not approached too closely
for the seed was too young to provide an adequate meal, you see

As spring approached
the life that began below the eyes
of the birds,
bears, foxes, and ants
suddenly appeared before the warming air and affectionate sun

The leaves grew stronger
and the worms circled closer to the now sturdy, mazed roots
that were teasing them further and further (for it was almost time)

But the worms, you see, were getting rather hungry
and hunger begot competition
and competition begot cannibalism

And so, the idea that once was a seed
within the confines of a dark, cold earth
blossomed with jeweled beauty weaved in its petals
much to the pleasure of the birds', bears', foxes', and ants' eyes

Wolf and Rabbit

As the night grew colder,
the young wolf's hunger grew stronger.
The hunt had been ongoing with no success—
it was on the third circle of the forest
that a fair rabbit made its way along the grass.
As pure as milk and honey,
thought the wolf, licking his sneered lips.
The rabbit stopped and fluffed her glistening white fur flirtatiously,
as the wolf began to circle its prey from afar.
The rabbit scurried along, knowing full well of the hunt now taking place,
and as the wolf picked up his pace,
the rabbit, rather charmed by the wolf's display of affection,
pretended to be in quite a scared hurry.
The wolf's heart beat ever faster,
but little did he know of the dance of nature.
And so, when the rabbit had decided
that the chase was proving too much for the panting wolf,
she simply stopped.
The wolf, confused, looked at the rabbit as it smiled.
"Why did you stop, my prey?" asked the wolf.
The rabbit said not a word.
With the rush of the hunt fading,
and seeing that the fur of the rabbit was, indeed,
yellowed and browned by nature's journey,
the hungry wolf slowly turned and left the rabbit to be.

Meteor Shower

So long now you have stared at the star-ridden skies
while the ocean beneath you
has been in awe of you
and you've paid it no mind.

The night behind you, there, on the boardwalk (remember?)
is carrying on with jovial energy
and has forgotten about you (as have you) …
but not the ocean
smitten, its flirtatious waves tapping at your feet.

The white sand beneath the moonlight shimmers with gemmed brilliance
twinkling individually to please every color your eyes can perceive
and yet, you continue to ignore the ocean's coyish gestures.

And so, the ocean has given up its quest for your attention
it has decided (as well as its inhabitants) that it will take you this night
it's just waiting for you to fall asleep on the white sand
as you listen to its waves' rhythmic lullaby.

Without Control

And the ocean pours water upon the body
for it has no respect for what it has killed.
The body lays there,
with windswept sand scattered top to bottom
and the blood gluing sand under the fingernails.

Two days ago this was
and still the ocean is without apology

Two days ago this was
and still the ocean is without apology

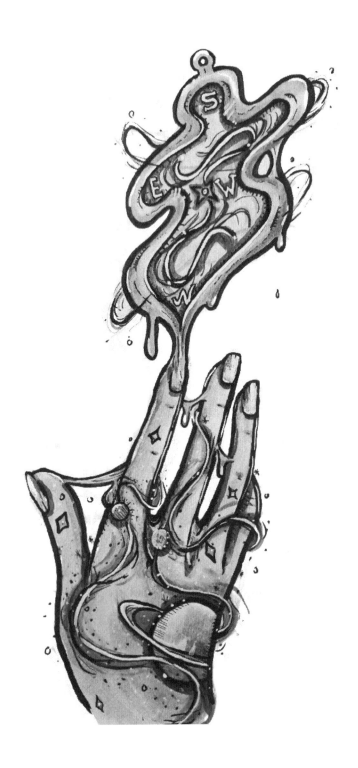

Condition

Once, there was that time
when nothing
equaled to such
and no questions were asked.

Came then a revolution of certain sorts
some did not like
many had not agreed.

Worries came
fingers pointed to one's self
—with one's own hand!
This was that time.

They had no answers yet
and with that, much confusion came.
North was South
West had no existence.

This was that time.

The revolution of certain sorts,
was in turmoil.

Medieval Justice

I never knew blood had this taste
and I never knew that my blood would be tasted
oh, my dear flesh has been seen

it has been found

and it has been searched.

Can you hold my mind for a while?
I've decided to take a break.

Dear friends,
hear me now for my speech is soon to be impaired!
Take forth the blood,
the flesh
and the mind
oh, the mind
and use with gracious respect
spread the word, spread the word!

Wolf in Sheep's Clothing

If I lie in agony
will you press a smile upon my grimaced lips?
Or will you
wipe my tears away (so that I can see what agonizes me better)?
If I fall into my mental abyss
will you see to it that I wander aimlessly there?
Or will you
guide me out of my mire (so that I can walk into another)?

Vietnam 1971

Running over rows of uniforms
sinking into blood-soaked mud
gun shots, rapid fire
bullets skim the ground
dirt scatters onto rotting bodies smiling at death
Heat from the sun glazing
the exposed flesh of his fellow men who lay
They won't stop biting!
Dizziness chokes his brain
heart pumping
gun in hand
first victim
screams
Tired souls of his brethren can't rest
With all this noise!
Sweat oozed from him
in this jungle of decay
of rot

The pageantry of war has begun

Have you ever touched your grave in tears?
Welcome to Vietnam

America's Fairytale

The princess has saddened her region,
as the dragon breathes no fire.

There will be no awakening kiss today
between the fair–haired gal
and the dark, handsome bachelor.
The prince-to-be
is hunting and fooling around.

And this time,
no animals will gather around her.
They are busy,
playing games of gamble
squatting with all their food, fat-bellied
with cigars in their mouths,
their fur uncleansed,
with smiles on their faces
as they breathe alcoholic exhales.

The mean old witch has broken her broom,
and her cauldron has been filled with dust.
Unable to fly, she lies on the floor with her savant helper,
laughing, clenching wine glasses in their hands and toasting.
Her evil sidekick raven has since been gambling
with the animals that reside near the castle.

The wicked stepsisters
wear Victorian lingerie
and work in the saloons.

The fairy godmothers have realized
that, indeed, no one listens to their teachings
and they spend their days in the bayou
with their wands resting at the bottom of the swamp.
They sit with their feet up, waving paper fans on their porch,
and throw parties with their neighbors.

Now– all good things must come to an end.

So, when the prince had failed in hunting
and grown tired of saloon girls,
he drunkenly walked to the princess
and kissed her.
She awoke from deep depression.

Her dragon flared flames from his nostrils with such gust
that even the far away isles took witness!
And the animals that had lost all their money
sat fat at first with shame and in debt,
but came to the princess in harmony
and she fed their hangovers away.

The witch had spelled a new broom
and cleaned her cauldron;
her savant helper, relapsed.

The fairy godmothers decided to teach in the day,
but would cut out the flying act due to their age.
At night, they would throw great ole bayou parties!

The stepsisters, filled with guilt,
remained in the saloons.

Waltz of the Dead

The moonlight's rays illuminated the pale faces
void of grief
void of happiness.
In an ossified dance under the moon,
the corpses embraced tightly in rigor mortis.

Within the shadows, the reaper sharpened his ax
(for it had become slightly dull, you understand).
The moon, no stranger to the acts that occur underneath it,
shined the path forward for the reaper's next steps.

Woodland Stroll

Children of the night
come slowly to feed
on what is left of the body

This decaying flesh
into the soil it goes
into the earth it seeps

no longer anything
except
bones left above ground as a memoir

It will be at some point
perhaps during a lovely woodland stroll
that someone will find these bones in horror

but say, what of death is horror?

Like a Virgin

The woman wore white as she entered the room,
but a liar she was!
Oh,
and they blessed her with great joy.
—*My, has guilt not ridden on her?*
Oh,
the groom-to-be smiled at her
as she made her way down the aisle.
And she gleamed in a white glow
that was fading the closer she came.
Oh,
and no one knew.
He took her hand with confidence
and put the circle of life on her.
—*Course it hardly fit.*
"She's nervous!" The guests merrily agreed and chuckled.
So, when night came,
no complaints from the room had to be tamed.
The husband's confidence boosted,
thinking he had done his job quite well.
Oh,
and the wife smiled
as she swore to herself never to tell!

The Prayer of the Hypocrite

To you alone I cry,
For to others I am strong.
To you alone I ramble,
For to others I am a smooth talker.
To you alone I reveal my fears,
For to others I am their fear.

Eve's Deceit

"Shh..." said the snake to a naked Eve.

"There are more secrets besides that of the fruit."

—What are they of?

"Your banishment will forever curse all those who are expected."

—This I know. Are you here to tease?

"Silence! Remember, I can tell you all and no one else will give
  you such privilege."

—Then tell me other secrets that He refuses to reveal.

"He already knows of your forthcoming demise,"
  spoke the snake.

—What else can you reveal?

"He sent me."

—And He led me here...

Kinda Busy Right Now - I'll be right out!

If you could please excuse me,
I'd like to take a few minutes to be in the throes of my mind
I'd like to feel the pain from my own thoughts.
Please excuse me for a few,
I'd like to crucify, if I may, my heart and feel it ache ever so
I'd like to feel its twitch that causes me to catch my breath.
It is quite the meditation
it is quite the folly of my depression
it is a quiet
suicide I participate in.
I need to take but a moment or two to
wallow in my imagination,
meditate upon my mind, and dwell in thoughts that lash me.
Please, just a second more now, that's all,
I need to drown myself in what lives only in my mind.

The Soul's Last Stake

His shadow moved opposite of him,
a sign that his soul was in distress.
As he walked,
head bowed,
to the river,
he glanced at inhabitants who made themselves hidden to the untrained eye.
They watched him in the moonlight's dim glow,
and at times, looked at each other with fret.
The torment within him grew as his shadow dashed to another direction,
only to be pulled back by the magnet of life within him.
The air was still except for his slow,
methodical
footsteps.
The river softly called his name
and hummed a tune that frightened the creatures.
As he stepped into the water,
his shadow was seen yearning for land (so it is now told).
And he allowed the currents to carry his body to where it so pleased
while he stared into wet darkness,
and his shadow, it too,
conceded to its fate.

The Journey

Listen carefully…
see the idol who stands between the deserts?

Do you see him?
My un-foe?
He stands with a rod
and he shakes with the waves of heat
that dance near your eyes.

Grab your throat now
Stop your pulse!
Fall down to your knees…
the heavens await you,
just forget your troubles.

Ah, these mindless whispers
changing focuses.

Listen!
Listen closely friend (so I say)
you can't be too sharp
with no mind in sight.

I've seen the moon shining bright
soldiers have gone and died in the fight.
Their heads crushed by the killing flight,
surround them now
and inhale their light!

Ha, ha! But they were just prostitutes of evil,
lusting after death
and now they lie in the battlefield,
their swords still raised in the air!

They said, "Justice!"
but their knives were already raised.
Oh, why must the angels' blood taste like this?
Agony cries with me over the lifeless body.

Tell me—
Does Satan dance in your dreams?
Does he ride on the silk carpet?
And does his tongue hold all
whom he has captured for eternal damnation?

Oh now!
Can you see yourself front and center?
Or are you too blind to see?
Question is this to be asked

Men of Pride
Men of Swords…
Would you hurt love?
For she is a woman with knowledge
from the fear of God (as they like to say)

Shhh…
even evil bows to this quiet voice
so then,
why can't you hear it?

Fallen Brothers

It was in the depths of the forest where
the eerie echoes of lost souls hummed in unison.
Their agony
I could hear deep within me.
I felt my soul sing for death to arrive,
as it had for my brethren.
Closing my eyes, I listened and swayed gently to the melody.

My last few breaths, breathed,
my last tears, fallen.
The hymn of woe
has consumed me.

Behind the Iron Curtain

Hey there, you
don't make fast judgments just yet.

Never mind the many strained faces
that sit on their concrete stoops,
watching you and wondering,
why have you arrived?

There once stood an eternal rainbow near the iron statue,
but war came
and famine drove the people to feast upon the rainbow.
Never mind the grayness of the skies,
of the streets,
of the skin colors,
of the stray cats,
of the cars,
of the dead grass,
of the buildings,
of the smiles,
of the hearts—never mind all that.
That particular river over there—
I believe it was where the king drowned and
where the prince was crowned.

Hey, you, see that corner where
the girls with golden hair decorated with red ribbons
sit and giggle?
The prince that was crowned was avenged right there!
Many trees line the side of this road,
for this is where parades for the rulers are held
every other street is bare.
You see,
the king doesn't walk through them.
Notice there are no houses,
just buildings;
they like equality here.

Hey, you there, listen,
this park...
why, this park is of much importance, they tell me,
and here's why:
Smiles in secrecy and laughs amongst
the best of friends are shared,
deep within, beyond the eyes of those
who sit upon their concrete stoops.

Secrets of Yesterday's Night

Tell me
of the stories from the past.
Tell me
of whispers that were heard in the night between lovers.
And tell me
how those whispers were heard by night's creatures.
I want to know the stories
of those who spoke under midnight moons
and of those whose dresses became dirty
from fogged nights and dewed grass.
I want to hear of those who kissed ever so slightly
between the bushes of kings' castles and
honored knights' rooms—
of those who knew that a fogged morning with rain
would come because they watched dawn rise
in front of them.
Tell me of the stories of those who left rooms to meet
with lovers at rivers
that echoed fish swimming.
And tell me of the tales
when the lovers would run
holding hands
through enchanted forests that watched them
as they only heard a slight rustle of wind blowing
between leaf holes.
Tell me how the night concluded
amongst much invigorating anxiety.
And tell me if, indeed, a fogged morning and rain was to come
the following day.

Dawn Feeling

The twilight hours
shimmer red-gold rays
Thick air, heavy with people's dreams
Delta state
silent frequencies slow-dancing in hertz
The thin veil thickens
as the sun rises
and all of our tethers to the galaxies and star clusters beyond
that form as we lie in state each night
sever for the day

BONUS

My 5th grade teacher gave a class assignment to write poems for what would be a collection of poems. I'd never written a poem before. Wind *is the only remaining poem I have from that assignment. The haunting regret I have for throwing away the other poems has never, ever left me.*

Wind

The wind whistles all day.

At day its beautiful whistle reminds people of a beautiful voice.

and through the shining sun the wind looks crystal and moves
gracefully through the sky.

But at night it fiercely changes to a tiger and howls, roars

and by the moon it looks like a shadow of evil.

Acknowledgments

A round of grateful applause to the following artists who graciously agreed to collaborate with me on this project. Thank you for making my words come to life with your beautiful art.

Ariana Paris - Becoming

Keremy Eason - Condition

Eli John - Waltz of the Dead *and* Woodland Stroll

Penny Dasi - 5 Minutes

Wendy Richmond - Eve's Deceit

Jessica Kelper - Wolf and Rabbit

About the Author

Natasha Ray James I grew up in Brooklyn, NY and wrote her first poem, "The Devil's Mouth," for a class assignment in the 5th grade.

Reach out and connect with the author:

Email: natashajameswrites@gmail.com
Socials: @natasharayjames

Made in the USA
Middletown, DE
18 August 2023

36670570R00031